William Winter, George Arnold

Drift

A Sea-Shore Idyl And Other Poems

William Winter, George Arnold

Drift

A Sea-Shore Idyl And Other Poems

ISBN/EAN: 9783744704366

Printed in Europe, USA, Canada, Australia, Japan

Cover: Foto ©Thomas Meinert / pixelio.de

More available books at **www.hansebooks.com**

DRIFT:

A SEA-SHORE IDYL.

AND

OTHER POEMS.

BY GEORGE ARNOLD.

BOSTON:
TICKNOR AND FIELDS.
1866.

CONTENTS.

	PAGE
MEMOIR OF THE AUTHOR	7
DRIFT	25
THE JOLLY OLD PEDAGOGUE	36
RECRIMINATION	41
INTROSPECTION	49
WOOL-GATHERING	57
THE TWO AUTUMNS	63
ALONE BY THE HEARTH	67
THE GARDEN OF MEMORY	70
AN IDYL OF OCTOBER	75
"ALL FOR LOVE"	80
THE BALLAD OF ROSALIE	83
TRAILING ARBUTUS	86
THE OLD PLACE	89
THE GIFT OF LOVE	90
MY LOVE	93
MINNIE'S ANSWER	95
AU COMBLE	97

Contents.

Sweet Impatience	99
An Autumn Joy	103
In Vain	106
Gone	108
De Profundis	109
A Farewell	110
Vale!	112
Expression	115
The Tryst	117
Among the Heather	119
The Lees of Life	120
Farceur de Poete!	121
Beer	123
Youth and Age	126
The Butterfly and the Poet	127
Cui Bono?	128
The Golden Fish	130
Ça m'est Egal	131
Gold and Purple	133
Parting	134
Then and Now	135
Summer Winds	137
Laziness	141
The Simple Rhyme	142
Meadow Sweet	144

Contents.

FAREWELL TO SUMMER	145
SEPTEMBER	148
THE HEART'S REST	151
THE SIREN OF THE ROSE	153
ON THE SANDS	155
FOUL WEATHER	157
APART	158
AT DUSK	160
SERENADE	162
VIA CRUCIS	164
CHRISTMAS EVE	165
NEW-YEAR'S EVE	168
JUBILATE	170
THE MATRON YEAR	171
REQUIESCAM	174
IN THE DARK	176

GEORGE ARNOLD.

———◆———

THE author of the poems contained in this volume was very dear to me as a comrade, and so I do not pretend to speak impartially of his character and his writings. During a period of six years it was my fortune to be associated with him under a variety of circumstances, and to participate in many of his pleasures and in some of his sorrows. Not many weeks have passed, since all that was mortal of him was laid in the tomb. It may chance, therefore, that tenderness for his memory and grief for his loss will somewhat color the language of this memoir. Affection is not critical. But, whatever be the faults of this attempt to depict the departed poet, I confidently believe that every appreciative reader of these poems will recognize them as the exponents of genius and of a remarkable and winning character.

George Arnold was born in Bedford Street, New York city, on the 24th of June, 1834, and died at Strawberry Farms, Monmouth County, New Jersey, on the 9th of November, 1865. The events of his short life were neither numerous nor striking. His parents continued to reside in New York till he was three years of age, when they removed to Alton, in the State of Illinois. There he passed twelve years of his boyhood, — happy, buoyant years, diversified by exercise and study, and blessed by free communication with Nature, amidst some of her most picturesque and inspiring scenery. There, doubtless, he laid the foundations of that profound love and genuine knowledge of Nature which he manifested in after years. He never went to school. His education was conducted by his parents, from whom he learned, in a happy home, those lessons of truth and fact, and those simple principles of action, which are the sufficient basis of an honorable life. Those teachings he never forgot; and, though his later years were not unblemished with errors, he was, from first to last, in all things and to all persons, straightforward, sincere, and manly. Nor was this result altogether due to early training. Simplicity and truthfulness of character were born attributes of the man. His nature was frank, gentle, and sweet, and all his impulses were generous and good.

In the summer of 1849 his parents removed from Illinois, and settled at Strawberry Farms, in the State of New Jersey. A Fourierite Phalansterie had been established there; but, at this time, it was gradually breaking up. Residing there during the next three years, seeing many social reformers, — some of them peculiarly rational, and some of them peculiarly eccentric, — and hearing continually of social reform, the impressible mind of the young poet took a philosophical bent, and began very early to speculate upon the difference between things as they are and things as they ought to be. This habit of thought continued with him to the end of his life. He was never a reformer, indeed, and for professional reformers he entertained a cordial contempt. His conviction appeared to be, — and it is, perhaps, as sound as any doctrine of contemporary social philosophy, — that "the world is out of joint," and that no mere human power is available to set it right. With his philosophy, however, — or his lack of it, — the reader is not concerned ; and I refer to his youthful acquaintance with reformers and doctrines of reform, only to explain that bias toward speculation which appears in certain of his poems, — notably in "Wool-Gathering," — and that independent mental custom of viewing all subjects through the eyes of common sense, to which may be attributed the vigor and freshness of much that he has written.

In the autumn of 1852, having developed a strong preference and natural aptitude for the art of Painting, he was placed in the studio of a portrait-painter in New York city. This was the beginning of his career as a worker in the fine arts. Experience proved, however, that he had mistaken his vocation. He speedily became a good draughtsman, and manifested skill and taste in the minor department of landscape-painting. This cleverness in sketching landscapes grew with his years, and afforded him great enjoyment. Several of his friends possess little sketches that he gave them, chiefly in water-colors, which, if much less complete as works of art, are often as characteristic of the author as even his poems themselves. Such a sketch is before me, as I write these words. It represents a square in an old German city. Around the square are quaint houses, with diamond-paned windows and staring gargoyles. In the background a vast cathedral lifts its spire toward the blue sky of summer, flecked with clouds of fleece. The lame beggar halts along in the shadow. Hooded monks stand apart, conversing. The whole scene is gentle, slumbrous, poetic, and suggestive. But it was oftener with the sweet or stern aspects of Nature that the poet's fancy held genial communion. He loved to think of quiet woodland places; of moss-grown rocks, and the bright green of creeping vines; of the musical purl and tinkle of lonely brooks; of thick-clustering, dewy roses; of the burnished glories of autumnal woods; of the wind among the pine-trees, on sombre autumn nights; of lonely beaches, whereon forever echoes the ancient, solemn dirge of the sorrowing, desolate ocean, mindful not alone of its own mysterious grief, but of missing ships, and vanished forms, and "wrecks far out at sea." His poems very beautifully manifest these moods of his fancy; and these moods also tinged his little sketches, and gave them a characteristic quality. But he did not succeed as a painter of faces and figures, and so he very soon abandoned the effort to become an artist with the brush. His early studies of Painting, however, were not wasted. Loving the art, and knowing its technicalities, he subsequently became an excellent art-critic. His criticisms of paintings, scattered far and wide in the daily and weekly press of New York city, are numerous, and are animated by genuine sympathy with noble and beautiful ideals, cordial appreciation as well of minor merits as of lofty conceptions, and a frank and hearty contempt for mere prettiness and charlatanism. He was unusually competent for the proper performance of this work, and, as far as is possible in ephemeral journalism, he faithfully served the art in which he had once hoped to win distinction.

The transition from the brush to the pen is not uncommon. With him it was natural and inevitable. Though his temperament was dreamy, his will never became the slave of dreams. He laid down the brush with a sigh; but he laid it down: and, thenceforward, to the end of his life, he worked with the pen, incurring the perils, bearing the sorrows, surmounting the obstacles, and enjoying the pleasures of the noble and fascinating profession of letters. His literary career extended over a period of about twelve years. In the course of that time he wrote, with equal fluency and versatility, stories, sketches, essays, poems, comic and satirical verses, criticisms of books and of pictures, editorial articles, jokes and pointed paragraphs,—everything, in short, for which there is a demand in the literary magazines of the country, and in New York journalism. The quantity of written material which he thus produced is surprisingly large. Much of it, of course, is of an ephemeral character. As is usual with men of letters, who live by their pens, Arnold was obliged to combine the profession of journalism with that of literature ; and in journalism, sufficient unto the day is the article thereof. But, while he wrote much for the moment, he wrote much also that will endure. He was not merely a journalist. The original mind, the large, warm heart, and the sleepless fire of genius often gave accidental worth to even his lightest compositions. In this way "he builded better than he knew." The reader of his " Mc-

Arone" papers, commenced in "Vanity Fair," November 24, 1860, and continued, in that and other journals, with but slight intermissions, until October 14, 1865, will especially appreciate the truth of this remark. Those papers, in which the Chevalier McArone records his own exploits and reflections, aim to excite mirth by their perfectly preposterous absurdity. (I except, of course, those written toward the close of the author's life, which are inexpressibly pathetic.) Yet, beneath their sunny vein of nonsense, runs an often perceptible current of strong thought and delicate sentiment, revealing the profound convictions and ardent, persuasive sympathy of a great nature. Similar indications appear in his stories. The poems, of the best of which (selected and arranged by the present writer) this volume is composed, reveal their author yet more distinctly. A subtle knowledge of the human heart, a quick sympathy with ideals of purity, innocence, and beauty, a thorough love for Nature, combined with real knowledge of the subject, — in reference to which most poets manifest laborious ignorance, — a fine appreciation of the holiest human emotions, a profound acquaintance with grief, an exhaustless impulse of tender humanity underlying the workings of a critical intellect, a sad, playful humor closely blended with pathos, a vein of religious sentiment, a manly spirit, proud and aspiring, yet capable of calm endurance and gentle resignation, — these qualities of mind and of character are clearly manifested in these poems, which are, moreover, with scarcely an exception, moulded and finished in deference to the dictates of thoughtful culture and severest taste. They do not attempt high, imaginative flights. Their conception was due to no merely artistic impulse. They were born in the writer's heart, and uttered naturally, in strains of simple and delicious music.

It does not seem necessary here to enumerate the various magazines and newspapers in which Arnold's pen found employment. He wrote for bread, and he sold his writings to whomsoever would buy them. It was noticeable, too, — especially so in his later years, — that he had no desire for literary reputation. He was industrious, in order that he might be independent of the world. He lived simply, because he could not afford to live magnificently. A poet, he was not lacking in luxurious and eccentric tastes. A young bachelor, he was not lacking in the careless liberality of jovial good-fellowship. Yet he accomplished a great deal of work, and he always did it promptly, and faithfully, and well. In this respect, and, indeed, in all respects, his private life was governed by the strictest principles of personal integrity. He had, despite his youth, a marvellous knowledge of the world, and he wisely chose to conquer his place in it, by ability, industry, honor, and cheerfulness. The principal motive of his conduct (and this, possibly, explains his indifference toward literary reputation, and his habitual neglect of the expedients by which commonly it is attained) was a desire to be, rather than to seem, — to develop his own character, to act ingenuously, to deserve the love of his friends, to surround himself with an atmosphere of cheerfulness, and thus to make the best of the serio-comic drama of human life. In this he succeeded. Those who knew him well, loved him dearly. They knew that he was genuine, that he scorned every description of imposture, and that his friendship — never idly bestowed — was, when once given, steadfast and true, alike in storm and sunshine.

This genuineness of character, revealed through the medium of a peculiarly cheerful temperament, — all the more winning for its latent sadness, — was the source of his peculiar personal influence, and of his capacity to inspire affection. He attracted the good side of every nature. Those who came in contact with him somehow exhibited themselves to the best advantage. He had none of the conceit of intellectual superiority, neither did he flourish his quill in the face of society. His manners had the repose that distinguishes the gentleman, and something of the autumnal ripeness and beauty which he so much loved in Nature, and of which he has written so well. Even his little superficial affectations were not unpleasant. He was fond of representing himself as an utterly selfish and heartless man, and of attributing selfish motives to the whole human race. He liked, also, to suggest the ludicrous side of serious subjects, and to dampen the fire of sentiment with the cold water of cynicism. But he wore the mask of Mephistopheles with an ill grace, and, toward the last, he laid it altogether aside. Gentle, simple, and affectionate, "a soul of God's best earthly mould," — such he appeared to me in those last days, and such I faithfully believe him to have been.

It is pleasant to remember that the closing days of his life were passed in the society of dear friends, and that he entered into his rest amidst scenes that were hallowed to him by tender associations of a happy and hopeful youth. His custom, for years, had been to spend occasional weeks of the summer and autumn at Strawberry Farms. Thither, accordingly, he went, in August last, having been ill for some time previously. His face, though it wore then a weary look, gave no sign of approaching death. Yet his thoughts had dwelt often upon that solemn theme, and I think he knew that the end was near. In spite, however, of sickness, pain, and despondency, his habitual mood of mind remained calm, and even cheerful. He continued to write for the press up to within four weeks of his death. The last prose article that he wrote was the last of the McArone papers, humorously yet very sadly expressive of a wish to be an Old Lady. The last poem that he prepared for publication was "The Matron Year." I think, however, that he subsequently wrote several little songs, which, being intended merely for his own amusement, are, together with many similar trifles, of earlier date, omitted from this collection. He had a happy aptitude for composing melodies to match his words, and, in private, he used often to sing his own songs. They were simple and sweet, and he sang them sweetly. Many an afternoon, in that golden autumn which was his last on earth, he sat alone in the parlor of the old house at Strawberry Farms, playing the piano and singing softly to himself. I picture him thus, as the end drew near, — his handsome face calm with the repose of resignation, his gentle, blue eyes full of a kind, sad light, his rich voice, soft and tremulous and low, breathing out his own glad hymn of faith in the protecting love of the Great Master:

> "To-day a song is on my lips:
> Earth seems a paradise to me:
> For God is good, and lo! my ships
> Are coming home from sea."

They have come home now, — all the high hopes, all the ventures of aspiration, that his soul sent forth, in the holy season of innocent youth. His dreams of happiness are all realized: his life that was broken on earth is fulfilled in heaven.

WILLIAM WINTER.

NEW YORK, January 21, 1866.

POEMS.

DRIFT.

A SEA-SHORE IDYL.

I.

I WEARIED once of inland fields and hills,
Of low-lying meadows and of sluggish streams,
Creeping beneath the trees that summer-heats
Had parched to dusty dryness ; and a dream
Of fresh, cool breezes and of salty waves,
Of azure skies o'erarching azure seas,
Of tangled seaweed from unfathomed deeps,
Came over me ; and so I left the hills,
To sojourn, through the riper summer-months,
Upon the shore.

      There, in a lonely house,
So near the breakers that their misty foam
Whitely enwrapped it when the storm raged high,

I let my summer-days pass idly by.
Yet not all idly : when the morn was fair,
And soft winds bore strange odors from the sea
Through open casements, oftentimes I wrote —
Weaving brief rhymes, disjointed, and, perhaps,
Too simple for the lovers of great poems.

  A ship went sailing from the shore,
   And vanished in the gleaming west,
  Where purple clouds a lining bore
   Of gold and amethyst.

  Poised in the air, a sea-gull flashed
   His white wings in the sun's last ray ;
  A moment hung, then downward dashed,
   To revel in the spray.

  The fishers drew their long nets in
   With careful eye and steady hand,
  Till olive back and silvery fin
   Strewed all the tawny sand.

Drift.

Again I trod the shore; again
    The sea-gull circled high in air;
Again the sturdy fishermen
    Drew in their nets with care.

The sunset's gold and amethyst
    Shone fairly, as I paced the shore,
But back from out the gleaming west
    The ship came — nevermore !

II.

After the first days, goodly company
Came to the lonely house beside the sea:
Bright eyes and tresses, voices of young girls,
Made joy within those somewhat mouldy halls;
And a piano, that had long stood mute
In the old parlor, on the landward side,
Grew musical and merry to the touch
Of jewelled fingers.   What rare days were those,
When my chief duty was to write a song,
As often as the brown-eyed Marian

Grew weary of my last! And thus our time
Passed, smoothly as a river-current flows.
Music and reading, strolling on the beach,
Gathering colored pebble-stones and shells,
And sea-weed from the rocks beyond the bar,
Were all our pastime.

  A flood of sunlight through a rift
   Between two mounds of yellow sand;
  Three sea-gulls on a bit of drift
   Slow surging inward toward the land:

  An old dumb-beacon, all awry,
   With drabbled sea-weed round its feet;
  A star-like sail against the sky,
   Where sapphire heaven and ocean meet:

  This, with the waters swirling o'er
   A shifting stretch of sand and shell,
  Will make, for him who loves the shore,
   A picture that may please him well.

III.

Ere the sun went down
We mostly loved to linger by the sea,
Where, seated on some wave-worn slab of stone,
We watched the furrowed waves that rose and fell,
Chasing each other down the beaten strand;
But when the shadows lengthened toward the east,
And the red glory of the sunset shone
Upon the light-house, and the fading sails,
The yellow sand-hills with their sickly grass
And inland-leaning cedars, we returned
To the old parlor; and, as dusk came on,
Sang to each other till the moon rode high.

    The light-house keeper's daughter,—
      Her hair is golden as the sand;
    Her eyes are blue as summer-seas
      That melt into the land.

    Her brow and neck are whiter
      Than sea-foam flying on the wind,
    Her mouth is rosy as the shells
      That strew the coast of Ind.

The winds caress her ringlets
  That down her neck in clusters stray,
And frothy waves flow tenderly
  About her feet, in play.

I love this simple maiden,
  She grows upon me more and more,
And — ask the moon who 't was that kissed,
  Last night, upon the shore!

IV.

At times, when moonlight danced upon the sea,
And all the air was musical with sounds
Of waters slowly breaking on the beach,
We sought the bar, and climbed its farthest rocks,
Against whose weedy feet the waves uprose
In phosphorescent foam ; and, seated there,
The maidens picturesquely grouped around,
We talked philosophy, or told quaint tales
Of most romantic sort, — of ghosts and ghouls,
Of strange things seen by those whom we had
  known ;

Drift.

Of strange things we, perchance, ourselves had
    seen ;
Of marvels told by ancient mariners,
The Maelstrom, and the heaven-dropped water-
    spouts, —
Or sadder tales, of wrecks far out at sea,
Of missing vessels, and of sailors drowned.

    The river down to the ocean flows
        By reedy flats and marshes bare ;
    And the leafless poplars stand in rows
        Like ghostly sentinels watching there.

    An osprey sails, with wings spread wide,
        Down-slanting from his even flight,
    To a sedgy spot, where the falling tide
        Has left some kind of drift in sight.

    A blackened mass, by the tide left bare,
        In the tangled weeds and the slimy mud.
    The osprey shrieks as he settles there,
        And a deathly horror chills my blood !

V.

So passed the summer, and we had our fill
Of lotos-eating by the ocean side ;
We came to know and love each pleasant spot
About the place ; the sheltered nooks where grew
Dwarfed flowers, whose downy seeds had come, mayhap,
Upon the wings of Autumn's winds upborne,
A thousand miles, to drop, and germinate,
In the dry sand ; to grow, and blow, and bloom,
And then to wither — 't were a happy fate —
In brown-eyed Marian's bosom. And we knew
Each craggy rock that overhung the sea,
Whence we could gaze far out across the waste
Of heaving waters, dotted here and there
With sails that shone and glimmered in the sun,
Like planets in a mellow evening sky.
Sometimes we went adventurously forth
When northeast tempests raged along the coast,
Flinging the white foam upward in great sheets,
Like hungry monsters rushing from the deep
To swallow up the land.

Drift.

    Then, bits of wrecks,
Odd timbers spiked with rusty iron bolts,
Fragments of masts, and empty water-casks, —
Sad débris of the storm, — came up next day,
Drifting ashore on smooth, unbroken swells.

 O cool, green waves that ebb and flow,
  Reflecting calm, blue skies above,
 How gently now ye come and go,
  Since ye have drowned my love!

 Ye lap the shore of beaten sand,
  With cool, salt ripples circling by;
 But from your depths a ghostly hand
  Points upward to the sky.

 O waves! strew corals, white and red,
  With shells and strange weeds from the deep,
 To make a rare and regal bed
  Whereon my love may sleep:

 May sleep, and, sleeping, dream of me,
  In dreams that lovers find so sweet;

And I will couch me by the sea,
    That we in dreams may meet.

VI.

But, while the pleasant season lasted still,
My friends deserted me for other scenes,
Leaving me lonely in the lonely house,
With memory's ghosts to bear me company.
Alone I sang the plaintive little songs,
That brown-eyed Marian had sung with me :
Alone I trod the path along the shore,
Where we so often had together strolled :
Alone I watched the moonrise, from the rocks
Where Marian had erstwhile walked with me,
To let the salt breeze, freshening with the night,
Play in her ringlets, and bring up the bloom
Of rose and lily to her cheek.
                                Alas!
If I should tell the whole of what I felt,
In waking these dear memories of the past,
This simple idyl would be lengthened out
Into a history of two hearts, that met —
That met — and parted!

Drift.

     Ah! the theme is old,
And worn quite threadbare, — not alone in books,
But in the hearts of men and maids as well.
But then, all stories that are true are old.

The breakers come and the breakers go,
  Along the silvery sand,
With a changing line of feathery snow,
  Between the water and land.

Sea-weeds gleam in the sunset light,
  On the ledges of wave-worn stone;
Orange and crimson, purple and white,
  In regular windrows strewn.

The waves grow calm in the dusk of eve,
  When the wind goes down with the sun;
So fade the smiles of those who deceive,
  When the coveted heart is won.

This seaweed wreath that hangs on the wall,
  She twined one day by the sea:
Of the weeds, and the waves, and her love, it is all
  That the Past has left to me!

THE JOLLY OLD PEDAGOGUE.

I.

'TWAS a jolly old pedagogue, long ago,
    Tall and slender, and sallow and dry;
His form was bent, and his gait was slow,
His long, thin hair was as white as snow,
    But a wonderful twinkle shone in his eye;
And he sang every night as he went to bed,
    "Let us be happy down here below;
The living should live, though the dead be dead,"
    Said the jolly old pedagogue, long ago.

II.

He taught his scholars the rule of three,
    Writing, and reading, and history, too;
He took the little ones up on his knee,
For a kind old heart in his breast had he,
    And the wants of the littlest child he knew:

"Learn while you're young," he often said,
  "There is much to enjoy, down here below;
Life for the living, and rest for the dead!"
  Said the jolly old pedagogue, long ago.

III.

With the stupidest boys he was kind and cool,
  Speaking only in gentlest tones;
The rod was hardly known in his school...
Whipping, to him, was a barbarous rule,
  And too hard work for his poor old bones;
Beside, it was painful, he sometimes said:
  "We should make life pleasant, down here below,
The living need charity more than the dead,"
  Said the jolly old pedagogue, long ago.

IV.

He lived in the house by the hawthorn lane,
  With roses and woodbine over the door;
His rooms were quiet, and neat, and plain,
But a spirit of comfort there held reign,
  And made him forget he was old and poor;

"I need so little," he often said ;
   "And my friends and relatives here below
Won't litigate over me when I am dead,"
   Said the jolly old pedagogue, long ago.

V.

But the pleasantest times that he had, of all,
   Were the sociable hours he used to pass,
With his chair tipped back to a neighbor's wall,
Making an unceremonious call,
   Over a pipe and a friendly glass :
This was the finest pleasure, he said,
   Of the many he tasted, here below ;
"Who has no cronies, had better be dead !"
   Said the jolly old pedagogue, long ago.

VI.

Then the jolly old pedagogue's wrinkled face
   Melted all over in sunshiny smiles ;
He stirred his glass with an old-school grace,
Chuckled, and sipped, and prattled apace,
   Till the house grew merry, from cellar to tiles :

"I'm a pretty old man," he gently said,
  "I have lingered a long while, here below;
But my heart is fresh, if my youth is fled!"
  Said the jolly old pedagogue, long ago.

VII.

He smoked his pipe in the balmy air,
  Every night when the sun went down,
While the soft wind played in his silvery hair,
Leaving its tenderest kisses there,
  On the jolly old pedagogue's jolly old crown:
And, feeling the kisses, he smiled, and said,
  'T was a glorious world, down here below;
"Why wait for happiness till we are dead?"
  Said the jolly old pedagogue, long ago.

VIII.

He sat at his door, one midsummer night,
  After the sun had sunk in the west,
And the lingering beams of golden light
Made his kindly old face look warm and bright,
  While the odorous night-wind whispered, "Rest!"

Gently, gently, he bowed his head . . .
 There were angels waiting for him, I know ;
He was sure of happiness, living or dead,
 This jolly old pedagogue, long ago !

RECRIMINATION.

I.

THE prime of summer is coming, and with it there comes, to-day,
A thought of another summer, whose garlands have faded away.
The tall laburnums are covered with tresses of yellow flowers,
As they were when under their shadow you used to loiter for hours;
And the blackberry's starry blossom and the buttercup's chalice of gold
Bloom bright in the ancient forest where you loved to wander of old, —
Where you loved to wander at even, but wandered never alone;
For a manly form was beside you, and a voice of manly tone

Told ever the olden story; the tale that you know
 so well,
You seem to think it the only one it is worth
 man's while to tell.
Come, sit you down here and listen; I have many
 things to say,
And though I am loath to blame you, yet pity I
 surely may.

II.

Ay, ay, you wince! I fancy you had rather have
 blame instead.
O girl! will you never learn wisdom? I had
 hoped your pride was dead;
But no, — it will last and flourish so long as vani-
 ties live, —
So long as you hunger for worship, so long as
 your subjects give.
It was strange that he thought you loved him; it
 was strange that he never knew
Your heart, except by the shadow that others
 mistook for you:

Recrimination.

But you went well masked, and no one, whether
    you laughed or wept,
Knew aught of the secret chamber where your
    broken relics were kept ;
You hid them so very securely the wisest had
    hardly guessed,
From your light-hearted tone and manner, your
    outer seeming of rest,
That your heart was a drear Golgotha, where all
    the ground was white
With the wrecks of joys that had perished, — the
    skeletons of delight!

III.

He loved you ; his soul was in earnest ; at your
    dainty feet he poured
The purest and best libation that human hearts
    can afford :
He dreamed of you morn and even ; he cherished
    the flowers you gave ;
And I tell you, though they are withered now,
    they will go with him to the grave !

Recrimination.

But you — how was it ? — you met him with
    marvellous glances and smiles ;
You wove your glittering meshes ; you compassed
    him with your wiles ;
You sang the songs he had written ; you talked
    in your sweetest voice,
Till he thought his bondage was freedom, and
    wore your fetters by choice.
Then a great joy flooded his spirit, and the yellow
    laburnum flowers
Heard wondrous vows and pledges, in the dusk of
    the evening hours ;
While there, in your heart, close hidden with jeal-
    ously watchful care,
Lay that strange Golgotha of passion, that arid
    waste of despair !

IV.

It is well that I know your story : I know that
    your first love came,
As of old came Jove to Semele, a splendid and
    fatal flame :

Recrimination.

And it left your heart in ashes, — dead ashes, that
    cooled and lay
A wearisome weight in your bosom, a burden to
    bear for aye.
Since then you have shown no mercy to any that
    circle around
The dangerous blaze of your beauty, for you no
    mercy had found.
'Tis for this I offer you pity, and blame you not,
    as I should
Had you still a heart that was human, with a
    human knowledge of good;
But the glass of your life is darkened, and darkly
    through it you see
Distorted and ghastly fragments of duty and des-
    tiny.
Yet you still can flirt and trifle, still live in folly
    and mirth, —
Ah! they say that revenge is sweeter than any-
    thing else on earth.

V.

But are there no better moments — better? or
    are they worse? —
When flattery loses its sweetness, and beauty
    becomes a curse?
When you come from the world of pleasure, the
    whirl, and glitter, and glare,
The tattle instead of wisdom, the perfume instead
    of air;
When the hot-house garlands are withered, and
    the gray dawn breaks in the east,
And the wine grows stale in the goblets that
    shone so fair at the feast;
When rouge hides paleness no longer, and folly
    gives way to thought, —
Do love, and life, and emotion still count in your
    creed for naught?
Do you never gaze in your mirror, when your
    beauty at daybreak goes,
And, pressing your throbbing temples, pray God
    to give you repose?

Repose! it is tardy in coming: when the bitter chalice is filled,
We must wait till the feverish pulses and the passionate heart are stilled.

VI.

There is one, that we know, thus waiting, — waiting and thinking to-day,
Perchance, of the happy summer whose blossoms have faded away:
He walks beneath the laburnums, but not with the hopeful pride
That made his world such an Eden when you walked there by his side.
O love! 't is a wonderful passion; it makes or it mars us all;
By love men may walk with the angels, by love the angels may fall!
And you — it has changed your nature, it has warped you, heart and soul,
Till you flee, with fierce desperation, the genii you cannot control.

What, tears? they are not becoming; let others
    such weakness show, —
The hall is garnished for dancing, the wine and
    the gaslights glow:
Go, stifle your sobs with laughter, let your eyes,
    like your heart, be dry,
And pray, when the ball is over, to be forgiven —
    and die!

INTROSPECTION.

I.

HAVE you sent her back her letters? have you given her back her ring?
Have you tried to forget the haunting songs that you loved to hear her sing?
Have you cursed the day you met her first? thanked God that you were free,
And said in your inmost heart, as you thought, "She never was dear to me"?
You have cast her off; your pride is touched; you fancy that all is done;
That for you the world is bright again, and bravely shines the sun:
You have washed your hands of passion; you have whistled her down the wind, —
O Tom, old friend, this goes before, the sharpest comes behind!

Yes, the sharpest is yet to come, for Love is a plant that never dies;
Its roots are deep as the earth itself, its branches wide as the skies;
And wherever once it has taken hold, it flourishes evermore,
Bearing a fruit that is fair outside, but bitter ashes at core.

II.

You will learn this, Tom, hereafter, when anger has cooled, and you
Have time for introspection; you will find my words are true;
You will sit and gaze in your fire alone, and fancy that you can see
Her face, with its classic oval, her ringlets fluttering free,
Her soft blue eyes, wide opened, her sweet red lips apart,
As she used to look, in the golden days when you fancied she had a heart:

Introspection. 51

Whatever you do, wherever you turn, you will see
    that glorious face
Coming with shadowy beauty, to haunt all time
    and space:
Those songs you wrote for her singing will sing
    themselves into your brain
Till your life seems set to their rhythm, and your
    thoughts to their refrain —
Their old, old burden of love and grief — the
    passion you have forsworn:
I tell you, Tom, it is not thrown off so well as
    you think, this morn!

III.

But the worst, perhaps the worst of all, will be
    when the day has flown,
When darkness favors reflection, and your comrades leave you alone:
You will try to sleep, but the memories of unforgotten years
Will come with a storm of wild regret — mayhap
    with a storm of tears;

Each look, each word, each playful tone, each
    timid little caress,
The golden gleam of her ringlets, the rustling of
    her dress,
The delicate touch of her ungloved hand, that
    woke such an exquisite thrill,
The flowers she gave you, the night of the ball, —
    I think you treasure them still, —
All these will come, till you slumber, worn out by
    sheer despair,
And then you will hear vague echoes of song on
    the darkened air, —
Vague echoes, rising and falling, of the voice you
    know so well,
Like the songs that were sung by the Lurlei-
    maids, sweet with a deadly spell!

IV.

In dreams, her heart will ever again be yours, and
    you will see
Fair glimpses of what might have been, — what
    now can never be;

Introspection. 53

And as she comes to meet you, with a sudden
    wild unrest
You stretch your arms forth lovingly, to fold her
    to your breast :
But the Lurlei-song will faint and die, and with
    its fading tone
You wake to find you clasp the thin and empty
    air alone,
While the fire-bell's clanging dissonance, on the
    gusty night-wind borne
Will seem an iron-tongued demon's voice, laugh-
    ing your grief to scorn.
O Tom, you say it is over, — you talk of letters
    and rings, —
Do you think that Love's mighty spirit, then, is
    held by such trifling things?
No! if you once have truly loved, you will still
    love on, I know,
Till the churchyard myrtles blossom above, and
    you lie mute below!

V.

How is it, I wonder, hereafter? Faith teaches us
    little, here,
Of the ones we have loved and lost on earth, — do
    you think they will still be dear?
Shall we live the lives we might have led? — will
    those who are severed now
Remember the pledge of a lower sphere, and re-
    new the broken vow?
It almost drives me wild to think of the gifts we
    throw away
Unthinking whether or no we lose Life's honey
    and wine for aye!
But then, again, 'tis a mighty joy — greater than
    I can tell —
To trust that the parted may some time meet, —
    that all may again be well:
However it be, I hold that all the evil we know
    on earth
Finds in this violence done to Love its true and
    legitimate birth,

Introspection.

And the agonies we suffer, when the heart is left alone,
For every sin of Humanity should fully and well atone!

VI.

I see that you marvel greatly, Tom, to hear such words from me,
But, if you knew my inmost heart, 't would be no mystery.
Experience is bitter, but its teachings we retain ;
It has taught me this,— who once has loved, loves never on earth again !
And I, too, have my closet, with a ghastly form inside, —
The skeleton of a perished love, killed by a cruel pride :
I sit by the fire at evening, as you will some time sit,
And watch, in the roseate half-light, the ghosts of happiness flit :

I, too, awaken at midnight, and stretch my arms
    to enfold
A vague and shadowy image, with tresses of
    brown and gold :
Experience is bitter indeed, — I have learned at a
    heavy cost
The secret of Love's persistency : I, too, have
    loved and lost !

WOOL-GATHERING.

I.

A PLEASANT golden light fills all the chamber where I sit,
The amber curtains close are drawn, and shadows o'er them flit, —
The swaying, shifting shadows of the honeysuckle vine,
Whose bare and leafless branches still about the porch entwine :
In summer, fresh and fair they grow, with blossoms for the bees,
But now in wintry nakedness they swing upon the breeze ;
Yet here, inside, 't is warm and bright, and I am quite inclined
To let this golden *demi-jour* make summer in my mind :

I sit with Jack — my terrier-dog — upon my lap curled up,
And, smoking thoughtfully, I seem to sip the classic cup
The Ancients called Nepenthe, — 't is a draught that brings repose
When one has lived or loved too much, — a balm for mental woes.
Yet, in this same Nepenthe cup, I know that some will see
Another name for laziness, — a common fault with me!

II.

Well, why not preach up laziness? I think it would be well
If some who cry it down a sin could only feel its spell!
The hard, ascetic natures — those who look for naught but Use
In everything one says or does — whose spirits are obtuse

To all the glorious gains of Art, to all the joys of sense,
And who cut their hard paths straightly by Poor Richard's eloquence!
Cui bono? Is there not a Power above the human mind
That works out all our problems, be they e'er so darkly blind?
And, after all, does Man, the unit, when his life is done
Ever look back upon its field to see the battle won?
No; I think not: we lay our plans, but when our life-star pales
We learn that human prescience inevitably fails.
Napoleon on his island, and Columbus in his chains,—
Are these the proud successes, then, for which we take such pains?

III.

Ah, many a one has started forth with hope and
    purpose high ;
Has fought throughout a weary life, and passed
    all pleasure by ;
Has burst all flowery chains by which men aye
    have been enthralled ;
Has been stone-deaf to voices sweet, that softly,
    sadly called ;
Has scorned the flashing goblet with the bubbles
    on its brim ;
Has turned his back on jewelled hands that madly
    beckoned him ;
Has, in a word, condemned himself to follow out
    his plan
By stern and lonely labor, — and has died, a con-
    quered man !
Look back, ye men of lofty aims, who in your
    youth aspired
To win some prize, — with love of gold or glory
    ye were fired ;

But now? let those who count threescore-and-ten
    full circles past
Tell how much they have gained and lost, — how
    much they hold at last!
Napoleon and Columbus, and legions more whose
    names
We never even heard of, — these were men of lofty
    aims!

IV.

So, in this softened, yellow light, with Jack upon
    my knees,
I find my good in being just as lazy as I
    please;
My pipe-smoke floats aspiringly, and that, I'm
    fain to say,
Is as much of aspiration as I care to see to-
    day;
Though Jack, disturbed by canine dreams, gives
    forth a sleepy cry,
And, full of lofty aims, prepares to conquer or to
    die;

No doubt some mighty, spectral rat glares through
 his visions dim,
Which Jack is bound to vanquish, or the rat will
 vanquish him!
Well, well, my dog, be wise, and all these high am-
 bitions keep;
Unlike poor man, indulge them only when you are
 asleep! —
What's this? I find that while in praise of lazi-
 ness I sang,
I've worked quite hard to write a metaphysical
 harangue!
Well, thus it is; consistency exists on earth no
 more, —
My pipe is out, my dog has waked, my laziness is
 o'er!

THE TWO AUTUMNS.

THE tall grass waves o'er lowly graves,
    The golden sunshine floods the meadows,
      And in the breeze, the willow-trees,
      That guard the tomb of Eloise,
    Wave to and fro, with flickering shadows.

    And here I sit, while bright birds flit
    Among the gravestones whitely gleaming,
      And muse away the summer day
      Beneath the vines' and willows' sway, —
    On that fair maiden's memory dreaming.

    O'er fields unmown the poppy shone,
    The earliest rose had hardly perished,
      When she confessed that in her breast
      Young Love was throned, a royal guest, —
    My image there alone she cherished.

The Two Autumns.

O happy hour, when from her bower,
With clambering grape-vines close entangled,
   We saw the moon of leafy June
   Rise calmly o'er the wide lagoon,
And climb the sky with bright stars spangled.

   Her deep blue eyes, like tropic skies, —
Not less profound, and never colder, —
   Were fixed on mine with gaze divine,
   And, golden as the German wine,
Her regal ringlets swept her shoulder.

   Her little hand, which scarcely spanned
With timid clasp my first three fingers,
   Her lip, her cheek, which bees might seek;
   Her voice — but, ah! mere words are weak
To paint the joys where memory lingers!

   The summer passed, and autumn's blast
Swept bleakly cold across the heather;

The Two Autumns.

The bright leaves browned, 'neath skies that frowned,
Then whirled in circles to the ground,
And strewed the paths we trod together.

O heavy grief! with autumn's leaf
They told me that her days were numbered:
She passed away, — her mortal clay
In death's pale beauty silent lay,
As calm as if she only slumbered.

I sit among the graves o'erhung
With many a slender-threaded willow;
The churchyard mould seems now less cold
Since, deep beneath, those locks of gold
Have found a soft and dreamless pillow.

About the tombs the laurel blooms,
I hear the bees above it humming,
The zephyrs sigh, in floating by;
They bring the scent of ripened rye,
And tell another autumn coming.

The Two Autumns.

Far down upon the horizon
A purple haze is softly falling,
    The fading rose of summer goes,
    And distant bells, at day's repose,
Unto my inner ear are calling.

Ah, dreamily they say to me
That those, who here are called to sever,
    Are elsewhere blessed with peace and rest,
    And I, unto this lonely breast
Shall clasp my Eloise forever.

ALONE BY THE HEARTH.

HERE, in my snug little fire-lit chamber,
   Sit I alone ;
And, as I gaze in the coals, I remember
   Days long agone.

Saddening it is, when the night has descended,
   · Thus to sit here,
Pensively musing on episodes, ended
   Many a year.

Still in my visions a golden-haired glory
   Floats to and fro ;
She whom I loved, — but 't is just the old story,
   Dead, long ago !

'T is but the wraith of a love; yet I linger
   (Thus passion errs),

Foolishly kissing the ring on my finger,—
    Once it was hers.

Nothing has changed since her spirit departed,
    Here, in this room,
Save I, who, weary and half broken-hearted,
    Sit in the gloom.

Loud 'gainst the window the winter rain dashes,
    Dreary and cold;
Over the floor the red fire-light flashes
    Just as of old.

Just as of old,—but the embers are scattered,
    Whose ruddy blaze
Flashed o'er the floor where her fairy feet pattered
    In other days!

Then, her dear voice, like a silver-chime ringing,
    Melted away;
Often these walls have re-echoed her singing
    Now hushed for aye!

Why should love bring naught but sorrow, I wonder?
Everything dies!
Time and Death, sooner or later, must sunder
Holiest ties.

Years have rolled by; I am wiser and older, —
Wiser, but yet,
Not till my heart and its feelings grow colder,
Can I forget.

So, in my snug little fire-lit chamber,
Sit I alone;
And, as I gaze in the coals, I remember
Days long agone!

THE GARDEN OF MEMORY.

THERE is a garden which my memory knows,
　　A grand old garden of the days gone by,
　Where lofty trees invite the breeze,
And underneath them blooms full many a rose,
　　Of rarest crimson or deep purple dye;
And there extend as far as eye can see,
Dim vistas of cool greenery.

Quaint marble statues, clothed with vines and
　　　　mould,
　　Gleam gray and spectral 'mid the foliage there:
　Grimly they stand on every hand,
Along the walk whose sands are smoothly rolled,
　　And borders trimmed with constant, watchful
　　　　care:
There Memory sits, and hears soft voices call
Above the plashing waterfall.

The Garden of Memory.

Old, faded bowers, with their rustic seats
    Of knotted branches closely intertwined,
    May there be seen the walks between:
Within their shade the dove at noon retreats,
    And gives her sad voice to the summer wind;
Around them bloom rich flowers, where all day
        long
The wild bee drones his dreamy song.

The garden stretches downward to a lake,
    Where gentle ripples kiss a pebbly shore:
    All cool and deep the waters sleep,
With naught the calm of their repose to break
    Save now and then the plashing of an oar,
Or the long train of diamond sparkles bright
Left by the wayward swallow's flight.

Within that garden Memory oft recalls
    Gay friends, who lived, and loved, and passed
        away:
    Who met at morn upon the lawn,

The Garden of Memory.

And strolled in couples by the garden-walls,
  Or on the grass beneath the maples lay,
And passed the hours as gayly as might be,
With olden tales of chivalry.

The younger maidens, each with silken net,
   Chased butterflies that hung, on painted wings,
   Above the beds where poppy-heads
Drooped heavily with morning dew-drops wet:
   In recollection still their laughter rings,
And still I seem to see them sport among
The statues gray, with vines o'erhung

One sainted maiden I remember well,
   And shall remember, though all else should
      fade:
   Her dreamy eyes, her gentle sighs,
Her golden hair in tangled curls that fell,
   Her queen-like beauty and demeanor staid,
And O, her smile, that played at hide-and-seek
With dimples on her chin and cheek!

The Garden of Memory.

O Edith! often have we sat at rest,
   And watched the sunset from the Lover's
      Hill,
When few, faint stars shone through the bars
Of purple cloud that stretched athwart the west;
   And Nature's pulse seemed silently to thrill,
While Night came o'er the moorlands wide and
      brown,
On dusky pinions sweeping down.

Long years have faded since those happy days,
   Yet still in memory are their joys enshrined.
   Tall grasses wave o'er Edith's grave;
Above her breast the birds sing plaintive lays;
   Yet still I feel her arms about me twined;
Still float her tangled tresses in the breeze;
Still sit we 'neath the maple-trees.

Thus may it be, until I too am gone!
   Thus let me ever dream of youth and love!
   And when the strife of earthly life

Is past ; when all my weary tasks are done,
   I know that in some garden there, above,
My angel EDITH waits to welcome me
Unto thy halls, Eternity !

AN IDYL OF OCTOBER.

JULIE, Mary, Billy, and I,
    Walked down the cedar-lane one day,
When the sun was bright in an autumn sky,
    And the trees with their autumn tints were gay ;
Down to the bridge our way we took,
    Past the chestnuts that crown the hill,—
Down to the bridge that crosses the brook,
    On the road to the cider-mill.

A year before, we had trod the lane,
    And then, half-jesting, ourselves we bound
To take the selfsame walk again,
    When another year had rolled around ; —
So, when another October glowed
    On shrubby hollow and wooded ridge,
It found us threading the cedar-road,
    And loitering on the bridge.

An Idyl of October.

The water swirled 'mong the oaken posts,
    In long, dark currents, eddying by,
And floating leaves, like shadowy ghosts,
    Were borne on its bosom silently.
The breezes dallied with Julie's hair,
    Where mingling gold and amber played;
Fair Mary's face seemed still more fair
    In the flickering shine and shade.

We feasted our eyes on the pleasant scene,
    We gathered leaves of a thousand dyes,—
Speckled with crimson, spotted with green,
    And shaded with hues from Paradise;
We sang and shouted, we laughed and talked,
    Till the woods were loud with our echoed glee;—
O, never a merrier party walked
    In a place more fair to see!

Last year, when under the autumn sky,
    Through these bright autumn woods we strolled,
We met a lassie, pretty and shy,
    Mayhap some seventeen summers old:

An Idyl of October.

A blue-eyed, bashful country maid,
    Who passed us, timidly glancing down,
Her blue eyes taking a deeper shade
    From their lashes long and brown.

I, who have ever been *farceur*, —
    Loving a merry word alway, —
Feigned to have fallen in love with her, —
    A new-born passion, to last for aye.
So, when we spoke of the cedar-lane,
    And plans for this year's ramble laid,
We wondered if we should meet again
    With the blue-eyed, bashful maid.

Then, I said that if we should meet
    With the country lassie, modest and fair,
There on the bridge would I kneel at her feet,
    And all my passion for her declare . . .
Well, as we came to the foot of the hill,
    Where the maples glow like a colored flame,
Down the road to the cider-mill,
    The blue-eyed damsel came !

But, alas for the ways of destiny!
　I spied some leaves so gorgeously hued,
Decking the boughs of a maple-tree,
　By a fence between the road and the wood,
That I vowed to have them whether or no, —
　Coveting beauty as some covet pelf, —
And, venturing where the ground was low,
　In a swamp I found myself.

There I gathered the prettiest leaves,
　Standing, the while, on treacherous ground, —
Such fair chaplets as Nature weaves
　When Autumn, King of the Year, is crowned, —
And there, alone, long after its time,
　I found a heaven-blue violet,
Gleaming up from the ooze and slime
　Like a jewel, foully set.

Many a leaf of orange and red,
　Gold and purple, scarlet and brown,
I found on the branches overhead,
　Or where the wind had rustled them down;

An Idyl of October.

Gathering these, no heed I paid
    To anything save my leafy load,
And the blue-eyed, bashful country maid
    Had gone, when I gained the road!

But Julie and Mary both were there, —
    Better than bashful maids are they, —
The blue-eyed lassie is not more fair,
    And not more modest, as I dare say;
I felt some pride, as surely I might,
    When I showed my leaves and my violet; —
Those autumn colors were wondrous bright,
    But those faces were brighter yet!

Whenever I see those leaves again,
    Pressed and varnished by Julie's skill,
I shall think of our walk in the cedar-lane,
    And the bridge on the road to the cider-mill;
And if e'er for the bashful lassie I sigh, —
    I, who have ever been *farceur*, —
I will see that she does not pass me by; —
    I'll wait on the bridge for her!

"ALL FOR LOVE."

ABOUT the pool the pansies blow,
    Fair they bloom in the summer sun,
With violets on the bank below
    And tangled vines that at random run;
The water is dark, and cool, and green,
    Its surface touched by misty rays
That slant the willow boughs between
    On sunny, summer days.

Across the pool the wingéd seeds
    Hither and thither lightly flaunt,
Blown from the shore of bristling reeds
    That gauzy dragon-flies love to haunt;
The shallows all are thickly set
    With lily-leaves and blossoms white, —
Their fragrant petals glistening wet
    With dewdrops, diamond-bright.

All for Love.

A silence reigns upon the air,
   Upon the pansies by the shore,
Upon the violets, pale and fair,
   Upon the willow, bending o'er;
The reeds and lilies silent grow,
   The dark green waters silent sleep,
Save when the summer breezes blow,
   Or silvery minnows leap.

Adown the path, that hidden lies
   Under the chestnuts on the hill,
Came pretty May with the hazel eyes,
   Whose father kept the neighboring mill.
Wild she muttered and long she gazed,
   Loosely floated her fair, brown hair:
Like one by a heavy sorrow crazed
   She laughed and whispered there.

Alas! her story was just the same
   That poets have told since poets have sung, —
Beginning in love, to end in shame,
   When hope grows old while life is young!

So, sighing wearily, down she strayed,
    While the sunshine slept on the silent pool,
To the flowery bank, and the willow's shade,
    And the water, deep and cool.

About the pool the pansies blow,
    Fair in the summer sun they bloom,
But the water is dark that lies below, —
    Dark and silent as is the tomb:
And I seem to see, wherever I tread
    The reedy shore where the willow stands,
The sorrowing wraith of one long dead,
    Wringing her ghostly hands.

The mill and miller have long been gone,
    The father sleeps by his daughter's side,
And many a summer's sun has shone
    Since hazel-eyed May lived, loved, and died;
Yet still in passing, the neighbors pause,
    And say, as they glance from the hill above,
"Let us forgive the child, because
    Her sorrow was born of love!"

THE BALLAD OF ROSALIE.

ROSALIE was strangely fair
   — Slow and weary the days go by —
With her splendid torrent of tawny hair,
   And her terrible, beautiful eye.

Love for her had made me blind,
   — Slow and weary the days go by —
Her heart was false as the summer wind,
   Her truest truth was a lie.

O, but she vowed by that and by this!
   — Slow and weary the days go by —
O, but her lips were sweet to kiss,
   And, O, but her heart was dry.

A chaplet once I saw her weave,
   — Slow and weary the days go by —

Her girdle pressed against my sleeve;
My cheek warmed to her sigh.

That night, wine in the cup was red,
  — Slow and weary the days go by —
The chaplet shone on Rosalie's head,
  So Roland's time drew nigh.

Song and laughter, peal on peal!
  — Slow and weary the days go by —
They could not hear the clash of steel,
  Their merriment rang so high.

Under the trees I left the knight,
  — Slow and weary the days go by —
My blade was crimson; his face was white;
  I wear good steel on thigh.

Morning came and the broad light shone,
  — Slow and weary the days go by —
The dancers and revellers all had gone
  When the sun climbed up the sky.

The Ballad of Rosalie.

Rosalie lay by the castle moat,
— Slow and weary the days go by —
A dark, red line across her throat.
— 'T were pity that she should die!

Her bright hair gleamed by the water-side,
— Slow and weary the days go by —
How she was loved and how she died
Nobody knows but I.

TRAILING ARBUTUS.

I.

WANDERING over the breezy slopes
   Where the trailing arbutus grows,
(That little flower that timidly opes,
While the wind of March still blows,
Its delicate buds of the palest rose,
And blossoms white as eternal snows),
O Love, we walked, and cheerily talked,
That breezy, blustering day,
Where the March winds blow, and the pink buds
      grow,
Wet with the morning's crystalline dew,
And far below us, stretching away
'Neath the sky with its spring-time azure hue,
The heaving, flashing, glittering bay
In solemn breadth and beauty lay!

II.

Sitting under the cedar-trees,
Inhaling their odor rare,
With the swaying, swinging, dallying breeze
Playing among thy hair,
Ah, still my fancy thy image sees, —
The checkered shadow and shine on thy face,
Lighting the place with a holy grace,
While thy voice was lifted in ballads old
Of maids who were fair, and men who were bold, —
Ah, heaven! thou too wert fair!

III.

The wind is blowing and blustering still
On the lofty cedared slopes,
And still on the southerly face of the hill
The trailing arbutus opes;
But alone I sit 'neath the cedar-trees, —
Alone with the boisterous, blustering breeze,
The flowers, and my own sad memories;
While the murmur that comes from the flashing seas
Whispers to me, all solemnly,

That love is only a vanity! . . .
Well, it has flown, as the winds have blown
Last autumn's dead leaves rustling down.
Each spring, the trailing arbutus grows
When the March wind blows, but love, when it goes,
Alas, is forever gone!

THE OLD PLACE.

I STAND on the shore of a moonlit sea,
    Under the stars of a summer sky,
And sad are the thoughts that come to me,
    As the sorrowful night-wind whispers by.

'T is the same old sea whose voices call,
    The same old stars, with their twinkling eyes,
The same old moonlight silvers all,
    And the same old solemn thoughts arise.

Naught in the scene has changed, for years,
    Waves, nor stars, nor moonlight fair;
And here in my eyes are the same old tears,
    For the same old hopeless love I bear.

THE GIFT OF LOVE.

"GIVE me," I said, "that ring,
   Which on thy taper finger gleams;
Sweet thoughts to me 't will bring,
When summer sunset's beams
   Have faded o'er the western sea,
   And left me dreaming, Love, of thee!"

"O no!" the maiden cried;
"This shining ring is bright, but cold:
   That bond is loosely tied
Which must be clasped with gold!
   The ring would soon forgotten be:
   Some better gift I'll give to thee!"

"Then give me that red rose,"
Said I, "which on thy bosom heaves
   In ecstasied repose,

And droops its blushing leaves:
  If thou wouldst have me think of thee,
  Fair maiden, give the rose to me!"

"O no!" she softly said,
"I will not give thee any flower:
  This rose will surely fade;
It passes with the hour:
  A faded rose can never be
  An emblem of my love for thee!"

"Then give me but thy word, —
A vow of love, — 't were better yet,"
  I cried; "who once has heard
Such vows, can ne'er forget!
  If thou wilt give this pledge to me,
  Nor ring nor rose I'll ask of thee!"

"O no!" she said again;
"For spoken vows are empty breath,
  Whose memory is vain
When passion perisheth:

The Gift of Love.

If e'er I lose my love for thee,
My vows must all forgotten be!"

"Then what," I asked, "wilt thou,
O dearest! to thy lover give?
   Nor ring nor rose nor vow
May I from thee receive;
   And yet some symbol should there be
To typify thy love for me!"

Then dropped her silvery voice
Unto a whisper, soft and low:
   "Here, take this gift,—my choice,—
The sweetest love can know!"
   She raised her head all lovingly,
And smiling, gave—a kiss to me!

MY LOVE.

THINE is a little hand, —
　　A tiny, little hand, —
　　Yet if it clasp
　　.With timid grasp
Mine own, ah me! I well can understand
The pressure of that little hand!

　　Thine is a little mouth, —
　　A very little mouth, —
　　　Yet, ah! what bliss
　　　To steal a kiss,
Sweet as the honeyed zephyrs of the south,
From that same rosy little mouth!

　　Thine is a little heart, —
　　A little, fluttering heart, —

Yet is it warm
And pure and calm,
And loves me with its whole untutored art,
That fond and faithful little heart!

Thou art a little girl, —
Only a little girl, —
Yet art thou worth
The wealth of earth —
Diamond and ruby, sapphire, gold, and pearl —
To me, thou blesséd little girl!

MINNIE'S ANSWER.

THERE 'S a certain girlish grace
    Hovers round thy form ;
Sits upon thy beaming face,
Sweetly blended with a trace
    Of a riper charm.
Should I say, " I love but thee,"
Minnie, were it safe for me ?

There 's a certain burning look
    Darting from thine eye, —
Reads my soul as 't were a book,
Searches every hidden nook
    E'en in passing by.
Shouldst thou fall in love with me,
Minnie, were it safe for thee ?

Then this loveliest of girls
    Raised her eyes to mine, —

Minnie's Answer.

Smiled, and brushed away her curls,
Smiled, — with teeth like matchless pearls,
  Lips like matchless wine, —
And she softly said to me,
  " I would take my chance with thee."

AU COMBLE.

HEART of hearts and pearl of pearls,
Dearest of all darling girls !
Can I make mere language say
How I love thee, night and day ?
Can I find, in head or heart,
Words to tell how fair thou art ?
Suns and moons may never shine
On a face and form like thine :
Rolling years may never see
Love more deep than mine for thee !
I have known diviner rest,
Softly pillowed on thy breast,
Than could ever haunt at night
Rosy couch of Sybarite ;
And no music ever fell —
Song of bird, or silver bell —
Half so sweetly on mine ear
As thy laughter, rich and clear !

Au Comble.

Now, since love is life to us,
Let us love forever thus!
Knowing that a brighter day
Shall behold us joined for aye;
For, to us, to love 't is given,
Here on earth and there in heaven.

SWEET IMPATIENCE.

I.

THE sunlight glimmers dull and gray
  Upon my wall to-day;
This summer is too long:
    The hot days go
    Weary and slow
As if time's reckoning were perverse and wrong:
    But when the flowers
Have faded, and their bloom has passed away,
    Then shall my song
    Be all of happier hours,
And more than one fond heart shall then be gay.

II.

But song can never tell
  How much I long to hear
One voice, that like the echo of a silver bell,

Unconscious, low, and clear,
Falls, as aforetime angel-voices fell
   On Saint Cecelia's ear:
     And it will come again,
     And I shall hear it, when
   The droning summer bee forgets his song
And frosty autumn crimsons hill and dell:
     I shall not murmur, then,
  "This summer is too long!"

III.

The trellised grapes shall purple be,
     And all
The forest aisles re-echo merrily
     The brown quail's call,
     And glossy chestnuts fall
In pattering plenty from the leafless tree
   When autumn winds blow strong:
Then shall I see
Her worshipped face once more, and in its sunshine, I
Shall cease to sigh
  "This summer is too long!"

IV.

Meanwhile, I wander up and down
The noisy town,
Alone:
I miss the lithe form from my side,
The kind, caressing tone,
The gentle eyes
In whose soft depths so much of loving lies;
And lonely in the throng, —
Each jostling, bustling, grasping for his own, —
The weary words arise,
"This summer is too long!"

V.

Haste, happy hours, —
Fade, tardy, lingering flowers!
Your fragrance has departed, long ago;
I yearn for cold winds, whistling through the
ruined bowers,
For winter's snow,
If with them, she
May come to teach my heart a cheerier song,

And lovingly
Make me forget all weariness and severance and
    wrong,
  Whispering close and low,
  " Here are we still together, Love, although
The summer was so long ! "

AN AUTUMN JOY.

IT is a fair autumnal day,
    The ground is strewn with yellow leaves;
The maple stems gleam bare and gray,
    The grain is piled in golden sheaves;
Afar I hear the speckled quails
    Pipe shrill amid the stubble dry,
And muffled beats from busy flails
    Within the barn near by.

The latest roses now are dead,
    Their petals scattered far and wide,
The sumac-berries, richly red,
    Bedeck the lane on either side;
A dreamy calm is in the air,
    A dreamy echo on the sea:
Ah, never was a day more fair
    Than this, which comes to me!

An Autumn Joy.

I see the stacks of ripened corn,
    The golden sunshine on the roof,
The diamond dew-drops of the morn,
    That string with gems the spider's woof;
An azure haze is hanging low
    About the outline of the hills,
And chanting sea-fowl southward go
    From marshes, lakes, and kils.

For many years, the autumn brought
    A plaintive sadness to my soul,
That shaded e'en my brightest thought,
    And on my gayest moments stole;
'T was sad, yet sweet, a strange alloy
    Of hope and sorrow intertwined:
This autumn brings me only joy,
    No shadow haunts my mind.

And why is this? The dead leaves fall,
    The blossoms wither, as of old,
And winter comes, with snowy pall,
    To wrap the earth so deathly cold;

An Autumn Joy.

The sea-fowl, strung athwart the sky,
   Still chant their plaintive monotone;
And why, when leaves and blossoms die,
   Should I feel joy alone?

O, ask me not, — I dare not tell;
   I must not all my heart disclose.
I think a fairy wove a spell
   About me, when decayed the rose!
Two gifts did dying summer bring, —
   Two symbols of undying bliss, —
Upon my finger glows a ring,
   Upon my lips, a kiss!

IN VAIN.

WHY were you kind, — O, why?
    Why did you smile instead of frowning,
When Love in Lethe's wave was drowning?
    Why were you kind, — O, why?

    If you had looked on me
With scorn, or wrath, or cold disdaining,
My love for you had now been waning;
    Why did you smile on me?

    Long had I loved; but Time,
Who softens all things, was beguiling
My weary heart, when, with your smiling,
    You came a second time!

    And now, alas! again
I bear love's chains, and, musing lonely,

In Vain.

Hear your sweet voice and see you only, —
   Why were you kind again?

   If all your love were dead,
Why did you kiss me, when we parted?
Do we "forget," when broken-hearted?
   Ah that I, too, were dead!

GONE.

THE summer was long and sweet,
   The roses blossomed for me
Over a porch where fairy feet
   Went pattering merrily.

All summer the roses smiled,
   Hiding their thorns from sight ;
All summer my passionate heart beat wild
   With a feverish love and delight.

Now, autumn's rain-drops beat
   On the casement, drearily ; —
The summer I found so long and sweet
   Has faded forever from me !

Under each thorny bough
   The roses are withering fast,
And my passionate heart beats slower, now,
   For the fever of love is past !

DE PROFUNDIS.

THROUGH the vague rifts in pearly clouds
    that lie
Along the horizon, 'twixt sky and sea,
A planet's trembling radiance gleams on high,
    Far, far from me.

The gentle breeze of evening loiters on,
    Faint with the breath of many a tropic tree,
But groves of sandal, spice, and cinnamon
    Are far from me.

O Love! I see thee glittering from afar;
    Sweet airs and silvery lights encompass thee,
But — like the spice groves and the evening star —
    Far, far from me!

A FAREWELL.

THE west-wind, laden with fragrance, blows,
   The dewdrops shine in the crimson rose;
— Is there something yet to tell?
Ay, winds must pass and dewdrops fall;
Naught that is gone can we recall:
   So now, dear Love, farewell!

Sweet lips prattle and laugh and sing,
White arms tenderly, closely cling;
— Is there something sad to tell?
Ay, the sweet lips shall silent be,
And the arms unclasp in their agony:
   So now, dear Love, farewell!

Then is there nothing that God has made
That will not one day fall or fade?
   — O Poet, in mercy tell!

A Farewell.

Ay, love shall reign in these hearts of ours
When eyes and lips and wind-waved flowers
   Have known their last farewell.

For love is purer than dewdrops are,
The winds go never so wide and far,
   And none may truly tell
How, when the close caress is gone,
And words are silent, true love lives on,
   Never to say farewell!

VALE!

O GENTLEST season of the changing year,
   Though thy bright days are past,
Our hearts will ever hold thy memory dear
   So long as memories last :
Gladly each year we see thy pageant glow
Through amber days with air like hydromel,
And now we sigh in whispers sad and slow,
   "Farewell, farewell!"

Through the dim vista of the forest nook
   Fall bars of shade and shine,
And o'er the shimmering ripples of the brook
   Swings the clematis vine :
The breeze comes faintly from the far-off sea
To linger in the leafy inland dell,
And sings October's dreamy monody,
   Farewell, farewell!

Vale!

The withered meadow-grasses, white and brown,
   Gleam in the autumn air,
Where shining stars of silvery cotton-down
   Go sailing here and there :
Decadence sits upon the fading earth,
Her flowers have felt the touch of Azraël ;
To blooming sights and chirping sounds of mirth,
   Farewell, farewell !

The day declines, and cloudy phantoms drift
   About the distant west,
Where many a purple peak and golden rift
   Welcome the sun to rest :
As goes this happy day, the season goes,
Its dying murmurs chant the autumn's knell, —
The solemn requiem of the earth's repose, —
   Farewell, farewell !

Fade gently, gently, in the western sky,
   O fair October day !
Let rustling trees give back the parting sigh
   Of winds that die away !

Vale!

Let the broad sunlight deepen into shade,
Let the kine homeward sound the tinkling bell,
To all thy glories that in twilight fade,
    Farewell, farewell!

The twittering birds may seek their hidden homes
    In the dark cedar-tree,
And hived bees, in honey-laden combs,
    Hum low and lazily:
O'er the wide landscape falls the shadowy night,
On field, and hill, and blue horizon's swell,
The sun gives forth his last expiring light, —
    Farewell, farewell!

EXPRESSION.

A HACKNEYED burden, to a hackneyed air,—
"I love thee only,—thou art wondrous fair!"
Alas! the poets have worn the theme threadbare!

Can I not find some words less tame and old,
To paint thy form and face of perfect mould,
Thy dewy lips, thy hair of brown and gold?

Can I not sing in somewhat fresher strain
The love I lavish and receive again, —
The thrilling joy, so like to thrilling pain?

Can I not, by some metaphor divine,
Describe the life I quaff like nectared wine
In being thine, and knowing thou art mine?

Expression.

Ah, no! this halting verse can naught express;
No English words can half the truth confess,
That have not all been rhymed to weariness!

So let me cease my scribbling for to-day,
And maiden, turn thy lovely face this way, —
Words will not do, but haply kisses may!

THE TRYST.

ON speary grass and starry bloom
    The tiny globes of dew are lying;
The broad moon rises through the gloom
    Of twilight haze; and night-winds sighing
In long-drawn whispers say to me,
" 'T is eventide... she comes to thee!"

A heavy fragrance floods the air,
    Where crimson roses climb and cluster;
Heaven seems more near, and earth more fair,
    The broad moon shines with holier lustre;
A white robe through the dusk I see...
O Joy! O Love! she comes to me!

PALINODE.
Athwart the west, where dies the day,
    A stormy rack of cloud is drifting,

And round the uplands bleak and gray
   The wind its mournful voice is lifting:
With every moan it says to me...
" 'T is night, but she comes not to thee!"

Sharp thorns now grimly deck the bough
   Where clustered once the crimson roses:
With roses once She wreathed this brow
   Where now a thorny crown reposes.
A bitter past alone I see...
Ah Heaven! she comes no more to me!

AMONG THE HEATHER.

WINTRY winds are blowing cold
    On the moors of purple heather
Where, in sunnier days of old
Hand in hand we idly strolled,
    Thou and I together.
But those sunny days are past,
    And no more we walk together
Where the snow, on every blast,
    Whirls above the heather.

On the dreary moorland, now,
    In the storm I wander lonely,
Longing — love alone knows how —
For thy kiss on lip and brow,
    Longing for thee only :
Life can bring me naught but pain,
    Till among the purple heather
Hand in hand we walk again, —
    Thou and I together!

THE LEES OF LIFE.

I HAVE had my will,
    Tasted every pleasure;
I have drank my fill
Of the purple measure;
    It has lost its zest,
    Sorrow is my guest,
O, the lees are bitter, — bitter, —
    Give me rest!

Love once filled the bowl
Running o'er with blisses,
    Made my very soul
Drunk with crimson kisses;
    But I drank it dry,
    Love has passed me by,
O, the lees are bitter, — bitter, —
    Let me die!

FARCEUR DE POETE!

SO, fare you well, true love, farewell!
    Did you think you saw an earnest woe
In the tear that just now flashed and fell?
    It was not so...
    I am a mere farceur, you know!

So, fare you well, true love! you said,
    One fair June night, when the moon was low
That you would love me, living or dead...
    I thought 't was so...
    But I am a mere farceur, you know!

So, fare you well, true love! though you
    Find peace and pleasure, here below,
I cannot: perhaps your heart is true...
    I hope 't is so...
    But I am a mere farceur, you know!

So, fare you well, true love ; we part !
The paths diverge whereon we go :
'T is said I carry a broken heart...
Can that be so ?...
I am a mere farceur, you know !

BEER.

H ERE,
With my beer
I sit,
While golden moments flit :
  Alas!
  They pass
Unheeded by :
And, as they fly,
I,
Being dry,
  Sit, idly sipping here
  My beer.

O, finer far
Than fame, or riches, are
The graceful smoke-wreaths of this free cigar !

Beer.

    Why
    Should I
    Weep, wail, or sigh?
    What if luck has passed me by?
What if my hopes are dead, —
My pleasures fled?
    Have I not still
    My fill
Of right good cheer, —
Cigars and beer?

    Go, whining youth,
    Forsooth!
Go, weep and wail,
Sigh and grow pale,
    Weave melancholy rhymes
    On the old times,
Whose joys like shadowy ghosts appear, —
But leave to me my beer!
    Gold is dross, —
    Love is loss, —
So, if I gulp my sorrows down,

Or see them drown
In foamy draughts of old nut-brown,
Then do I wear the crown,
   Without the cross!

YOUTH AND AGE.

YOUTH hath many charms, —
    Hath many joys, and much delight ;
Even its doubts, and vague alarms,
    By contrast make it bright :
And yet — and yet — forsooth,
I love Age as well as Youth !

Well, since I love them both,
    The good of both I will combine, —
In women, I will look for Youth,
    And look for Age, in wine :
And then — and then — I 'll bless
This twain that give me happiness !

THE BUTTERFLY AND THE POET.

THE BUTTERFLY.

ON gorgeous wings he floateth along,
    Little for this world careth he,
Save for the wild bee's somnolent song
    And the sweets in flowers that be :
He sippeth to-day from the Lily's bell ;
To-morrow, he loveth the Rose as well.

THE POET.

ON gorgeous dreams he floateth along,
    Nothing for this world careth he,
Save for the maidens' laughter and song
    And the sweets on their lips that be :
To-day, blonde Edith he loveth well ; . . .
To-morrow, 't is brown-eyed Isabel.

CUI BONO?

A HARMLESS fellow, wasting useless days,
    Am I: I love my comfort and my leisure:
Let those who wish them, toil for gold and praise,
    To me, this summer-day brings more of pleasure.

So, here upon the grass I lie at ease,
    While solemn voices from the Past are calling,
Mingled with rustling whispers in the trees,
    And pleasant sounds of water idly falling.

There was a time when I had higher aims
    Than thus to lie among the flowers, and listen
To lisping birds, or watch the sunset's flames
    On the broad river's surface glow and glisten.

There was a time, perhaps, when I had thought
    To make a name, a home, a bright existence:

But time has shown me that my dreams were naught
    Save a mirage that vanished with the distance.

Well, it is gone : I care no longer now
    For fame, for fortune, or for empty praises ;
Rather than wear a crown upon my brow,
    I 'd lie forever here among the daisies.

So you, who wish for fame, good friend, pass by :
    With you I surely cannot think to quarrel :
Give me peace, rest, this bank whereon I lie,
    And spare me both the labor and the laurel !

THE GOLDEN FISH.

L OVE is a little golden fish,
    Wondrous shy... ah, wondrous shy...
You may catch him, if you wish,
He might make a dainty dish...
    But I...
    Ah, I've other fish to fry!

For when I try to snare this prize,
   Earnestly, and patiently,
All my skill the rogue defies,
Lurking safe in Aimée's eyes...
    So you see,
    I am caught, and love goes free!

ÇA M'EST EGAL!

O, I WAS made for the present time!
    The present time was made for me!
I sing my song or weave my rhyme,
    From fear of future troubles free, —
    For they are naught to me!

'T is well with me at the present day:
    My brown-eyed Alice sits by me:
'T is true the moments pass away,
    And time is fleeting silently, —
    But that is naught to me!

I will not mourn for the silent past,
    Though pleasures fine it brought to me;
The present moments cannot last,
    But if they leave no vacancy,
    The past is naught to me!

Ça m'est Egal!

I fill a bowl with rose-foamed wine,
   My Alice quaffs a health to me;
The present joyous day is mine,
     The coming woe I cannot see, —
   So that is naught to me!

And thus I find in the present time,
   That life is fresh and sweet to me;
I still will sit and weave my rhyme;
     The future soon will present be, —
   And bring new joys to me!

GOLD AND PURPLE.

IN this little, old-fashioned garden of mine
    Poppies, and pinks, and pansies grow ;
Yellow of gold and purple of wine
    Within their clustering blossoms glow ;
And a purple ribbon is fluttering there,
From tangled ringlets of golden hair.

I love the pansies, poppies, and pinks,
    Their glistening eyes with the dewdrops wet :
I love them, — but in the garden, methinks,
    There is something that I love better yet ;
For a purple ribbon is fluttering there,
From tangled tresses of golden hair.

PARTING.

WHITE and small was the hand I pressed
    Behind the rose-covered cottage door,
While the moon rode low in the azure west,
And the tremulous vines, by the wind caressed,
    Cast flickering shadows over the floor, —
Swinging, swaying, and sighing lowly,
"Perfect love is the one thing holy!"

Rosy and ripe were the lips I pressed
    Behind the rose-covered cottage door,
While the orioles slept in their downy nest
That swung in the vines, by the wind caressed,
    Casting weird shadows over the floor, —
But the wind in the tremulous vines sang ever,
"Love must perish and hearts must sever!"

THEN AND NOW.

YOU loved me once, ... ah, well I knew it then!
   One night you kissed me, underneath the
      roses,
And said that we must never kiss again ...
That was the parting ... that strange moment,
      when
   The heart its weakness and its strength dis-
      closes ...
I knew you loved me then!

You love me yet ... ah, well I know it now!
   By these few stolen kisses, sad as tender,
That give my spirit strength, I know not how,
Falling like benisons on lip and brow, ,
   To fill my soul with mingled gloom and splen-
      dor ...
I know you love me now!

As then, and now, O let it be for aye!
Let those dear lips still tell the sweet old story.
Let these kind kisses still drive grief away,
Lighten my heavy cross from day to day,
And make my crown of thorns a crown of glory
For ever and for aye!

SUMMER WINDS.

I.

SUMMER winds, whispering over the rye,
  Kissing the roses and hurrying by,
  Where have ye latest been, O where?
  Merrily tangling my maiden's hair, —
Wafting the tresses over her cheek, —
Playing among them at hide and seek,
  Or trying with delicate scents of the south
  To rival the breath from her own sweet mouth?
Tell me, summer winds, fresh and fair,
Where have ye latest been, O where?

But the balmy breezes floated away,
Daintily sighing, — no word said they.

II.
Bear ye no word from my maiden to me?
Did she not whisper her love to ye?

Ah, well do I know that her fondest dream
By the sun's warm light or the moon's pale beam
Is ever of me, and the love she bears
Oft breaks from her sweet lips, unawares.
Has she not murmured some tender word
That ye, as ye wafted by, have heard?
Tell me, summer winds, frolic and free,
Bring ye no message from her to me?

But the balmy breezes frolicked away,
Daintily sighing, — no word said they.

III.

O faithless winds, since thus ye are still,
And bring no message my heart to thrill,
I will send ye again to my maiden's side
To tell her I'll meet her at eventide;
Then fly, fly fast o'er the waving rye, —
The roses are lovely, but pass them by, —
Bid them to wait for the kisses they crave,
And linger not on the rivulet's wave:
Haste, O summer winds, sighing above,
Tell her this night shall she meet her love!

The balmy breezes floated away,
And the roses wept that they would not stay.

IV.

Over the hill the summer winds sped,
Whirling and eddying overhead,
   Waving the moss on the cottage eaves,
   Rustling the feathery locust-leaves,
Brushing the dew-drops lingering yet
On the odorous blooms of the mignonette,
   Till they reached a garden kept with care,
   And found a beautiful maiden there,
Alone in an arbor, where misty lines
Of sunshine fell through the tangled vines.

Then the balmy breezes sought her ear,
And the words they whispered were low but clear.

V.

They raised the tresses of gold and brown
That over her snowy neck swept down,
   They said, in a musical, breezy voice,
   "Thy lover is coming, sweet child, rejoice!

When Hesperus' light in the west grows dim,
Thy lover will seek thee ; be ready for him !"
    The maiden heard, and a rosy glow
    Flushed up to her cheek from her heart below,
And e'en as the summer winds fleeted by
They bore from her bosom a gentle sigh.

Then the balmy breezes floated away,
And soon 'mong the rose-leaves nestled they.

LAZINESS.

MY window-curtain sweeps
  To and fro, in the lazy breeze,
As sea-weeds swing and sway in the deeps
  Of southern summer seas.

The lazy sunshine sleeps
  On the rose and snow of the apple-trees,
And lazy spring my spirit steeps
  In a lotos-dream of ease.

THE SIMPLE RHYME.

BENEATH the blue of summer skies,
    Among the flowers of summer-time,
With loitering steps and half-closed eyes
    I walk, and weave a simple rhyme.

The summer breezes go and come,
    And blowing, musical and free,
Bring sounds of bees that idly hum
    About the tangled briony.

Beneath the blue of summer skies,
    Among the flowers of summer-time,
With loitering steps and dreamy eyes,
    Fair maids shall sing my simple rhyme,

And may its echoes go and come
As fresh, as musical, as free,
As honey-bees that idly hum
About the tangled briony!

MEADOW-SWEET.

THE creamy banks of meadow-sweet
    Along the mill-stream's margin grow,
Where honey-bees with pollened feet
    Hum softly to and fro.

The sound is sweet, the fragrance rare,
    As summer breezes float along,
And round me all the summer air
    Is full of scent and song.

O, what to me are wealth and rank?
    O, what are men, and their deceit?
While I lie here, on the mill-stream's bank,
    Among the meadow-sweet!

FAREWELL TO SUMMER.

SUMMER is fading; the broad leaves that grew
    So freshly green, when June was young, are
        falling;
And, all the whisper-haunted forest through,
    The restless birds in saddened tones are calling,
From rustling hazel copse and tangled dell,
    " Farewell, sweet Summer,
        Fragrant, fruity Summer,
            Sweet, farewell!"

Upon the windy hills, in many a field,
    The honey-bees hum slow, above the clover,
Gleaning the latest sweets its blooms may yield,
    And, knowing that their harvest-time is over,
Sing, half a lullaby and half a knell,
    " Farewell, sweet Summer,
        Honey-laden Summer,
            Sweet, farewell!"

Farewell to Summer.

The little brook that babbles 'mid the ferns,
    O'er twisted roots and sandy shallows playing,
Seems fain to linger in its eddied turns,
    And with a plaintive, purling voice, is saying,
(Sadder and sweeter than my song can tell,)
    "Farewell, sweet Summer,
        Warm and dreamy Summer,
            Sweet, farewell!"

The fitful breeze sweeps down the winding lane
    With gold and crimson leaves before it flying;
Its gusty laughter has no sound of pain,
    But in the lulls it sinks to gentle sighing,
And mourns the Summer's early broken spell, —
    "Farewell, sweet Summer,
        Rosy, blooming Summer,
            Sweet, farewell!"

So bird, and bee, and brook, and breeze make moan,
    With melancholy song their loss complaining.
I too must join them, as I walk alone

Farewell to Summer.

Among the sights and sounds of Summer's wan-
 ing ...
I too have loved the season passing well ...
 So, farewell, Summer,
  Fair but faded Summer,
   Sweet, farewell!

SEPTEMBER.

SWEET is the voice that calls
    From babbling waterfalls
In meadows where the downy seeds are flying ;
    And soft the breezes blow,
    And eddying come and go,
In faded gardens where the rose is dying.

    Among the stubbled corn
    The blithe quail pipes at morn,
The merry partridge drums in hidden places,
    And glittering insects gleam
    Above the reedy stream
Where busy spiders spin their filmy laces.

    At eve, cool shadows fall
    Across the garden wall,
And on the clustered grapes to purple turning,

September.

And pearly vapors lie
Along the eastern sky,
Where the broad harvest-moon is redly burning.

Ah, soon on field and hill
The winds shall whistle chill,
And patriarch swallows call their flocks together
To fly from frost and snow,
And seek for lands where blow
The fairer blossoms of a balmier weather.

The pollen-dusted bees
Search for the honey-lees
That linger in the last flowers of September,
While plaintive mourning doves
Coo sadly to their loves
Of the dead summer they so well remember.

The cricket chirps all day,
"O fairest Summer, stay!"
The squirrel-eyes askance the chestnuts browning;

September.

    The wild-fowl fly afar
    Above the foamy bar
And hasten southward ere the skies are frowning.

    Now comes a fragrant breeze
    Through the dark cedar-trees
And round about my temples fondly lingers,
      In gentle playfulness,
      Like to the soft caress
Bestowed in happier days by loving fingers.

    Yet, though a sense of grief
    Comes with the falling leaf,
And memory makes the summer doubly pleasant,
      In all my autumn dreams
      A future summer gleams
Passing the fairest glories of the present!

THE HEART'S REST.

[GERMAN.]

THE wind is idly blowing
   And spilling its perfume rare;
The brook with its ceaseless flowing,
   Is singing a quaint old air.

But night o'er nature comes stealing,
   And the wind will die on the hill:
Cold Winter's ice, congealing,
   Will hush the song of the rill.

My heart, like the wind, is moaning,
   The day seems heavy and long,
And memory's voice is droning
   A sad, monotonous song.

The Heart's Rest.

But, heart, thou shalt rest at even,
    And memory's voice shall cease,
For the weary find rest in heaven,
    And the troubled shall be at peace.

THE SIREN OF THE ROSE.

ONCE in an ancient garden I found a maid,
    Who sat, entranced by perfumes from many
        a blossom ;
Between the trees the sunlight, down-gliding,
    played
    Upon her shining tresses and snowy bosom :
She was so fair, I fancied she could but be
    Some fairy thing, immortal, and more than
        human ;
I gave her purest lilies : she answered me,
    „ Die Rose ist die schönste von allen Blumen ! "

I offered her bright pansies, and meadow-sweet,
    Great daffodils, and tulips in regal splendor,
I laid green wreaths of laurel before her feet,
    And while I knelt her glances were dark and
        tender :

Yet still she shook, though gently, her beauteous
   head ;
Who had resisted, surely, were one of few men !
And meekly still, in answer, she smiled and said,
   „ Die Rose ist die schönste von allen Blumen ! "

I gazed about me, troubled : lo ! on my breast
   A crimson rose shone fairly, half bud, half
      blossom ;
I laid it, in its beauty, among the rest. . .
   She placed the fragrant secret within her bosom !
" Ah ! with it," cried I, stricken, " thou hast my
      heart !
   I love thee, be thou fairy, or mortal woman ! "
She whispered : " We are wedded, no more to part . . .
Die Rose ist die schönste von allen Blumen ! "

ON THE SANDS.

I MET Jessie Leigh
   On the sands;
Sweetly she smiled on me,
While breezes from the sea
   Brought dreamy odors as from distant lands,
And the warm sunshine fell
O'er weed, and pebble, and shell,
   Upon the sands.

I sat with Jessie Leigh
   On the sands;
Very fair was she,
And very kind to me;
   I kissed her forehead, and her dainty hands,
While the white moon above
Witnessed our vows of love,
   Upon the sands.

I saw Jessie Leigh
   On the sands;
Cold and white lay she,
Drowned in the cruel sea,
   Her fair hair floating in dishevelled strands.
Would God I too had died,
And slept there by her side,
   Upon the sands!

FOUL WEATHER.

THE rain, upon the sodden grass,
    Is beating, beating wearily;
Gray clouds of mist, like phantoms, pass,
    And the salt, wet wind wails drearily,
As it brings to me, from the shore afar,
The dirge of the surf on the outer bar.

My heart, within my fevered breast,
    Is beating, beating wearily,
And memory, with a sad unrest,
    Wails through its chambers drearily,
Till I almost wish that the surf afar
Were singing my dirge on the outer bar.

APART.

A WAVE, mid-ocean, sorrowed for the shore,
    "O, may I never see the smiling land?
Must I, then, break, and be a wave no more,
    Before I kiss the sand?"

A caged bird sang from early dawn till late,
    "Must I in gilded loneliness still pine,
Nor know the joy of nesting with my mate,
    Her rosy beak to mine?"

A tropic blossom drooped its bell above
    The northern loam: "O, may I never strew
My thirsty pollen in the blooms I love,
    And drink their honeyed dew?"

So I, O Love! am yearning for thy smile;
    So, mateless, I a sorrowing song upraise;

So for thy bloom I thirst and sigh, the while
    I count the weary days!

But though the wave may break its foamy crest,
    The bird be captive till its days are done,
The lonely blossom wither all unblest,
    Our lives shall yet be one!

AT DUSK.

A SHADOWY dance of ghostly images
    By the red firelight on the wall is flung,
And ivory fingers on the ivory keys
    Wake the old waltz we loved when love was young.

On music is poetic fancy fed,
    And these soft strains bring many a thought to me,
Sad with the knell of hopes and pleasures dead,
    Sweet with the promise of new joys to be.

In the warm firelight's glow thy shining hair
    Seems half transmuted into precious gold,
And, faintly falling on the dusky air,
    The olden cadence wakes the dream of old.

At Dusk.

O Love! the cup was bitter, but its lees
   Are sweet as honeyed dew in Hybla's flowers,
And all our days are fraught with prophecies
   Of sweeter draughts to come in future hours.

SERENADE.

I HEAR the dry-voiced insects call,
   And "Come," they say, "the night grows brief!"
I hear the dew-drops pattering fall
   From leaf to leaf,— from leaf to leaf.

Your night-lamp glimmers fitfully;
   I watch below, you sleep above;
Yet on your blind I seem to see
   Your shadow, love, — your shadow, love!

The roses in the night-wind sway,
   Their petals glistening with the dew;
As they are longing for the day,
   I long for you, — I long for you

But you are in the land of dreams;
   Your eyes are closed, your gentle breath

Serenade.

So faintly comes, your slumber seems
 Almost like death, — almost like death!

Sleep on; but may my music twine
 Your sleep with strands of melody,
And lead you, gentle love of mine,
 To dream of me, — to dream of me!

VIA CRUCIS.

WHO treads the path of love and loss,
    With humble steps and head bowed down,
May bear on earth the heaviest cross,
    But wears in heaven the brightest crown.

Then let us bless the weary way,
    The cross, the thorn, the cruel rod,
That lift us from our gods of clay
    To know the true, the living God!

CHRISTMAS EVE.

O SUCH a wee, white stocking
    As Clare by the fireside hung,
When the Christmas-eve fire was waning
    And the Christmas-eve hymn was sung.
O, such a wee, wee stocking,
    So dainty, so snowily white,
That she hung on a branch of green holly,
    Ere bidding us all "Good-night!"

What shall I put in her stocking?
    Some pleasant book? or a rhyme?
Shall I write her a gentle lyric
    Of love and the holiday time?
No: books are better for scholars;
    At best they are silent friends;
My rhymes, — alas! they are many,
    But there their virtue ends.

Then what shall I put in the stocking
    That the hazel-eyed maiden hung
On a twig of red-berried holly
    When the Christmas-eve hymn was sung?
Let me put my heart in the stocking
    — A fitting gift it would be! —
But my heart is large, — it is boundless, —
    And the stocking is dainty and wee.

Well, here is the ring on my finger,
    I've worn it many a year;
'T was the gift of an ancient comrade
    Whose memory I hold dear.
Yet nothing on earth I treasure
    So much that she might not say, —
"O, give me this if you love me," —
    And bear it — a trophy — away!

So I drop my ring in the stocking
    — She knows it is mine full well.
(Good comrade, I prithee, forgive me!
    None other my love could tell.)

I drop my ring in the stocking
    So dainty, so snowy, so small, —
O Clare, as I cherish and love thee,
    May God love and cherish us all !.

Ah me ! my heart is boundless,
    The stocking is dainty and wee ;
But love has a wonderful magic
    And wonderful power on me :
When I dropped my ring in the stocking,
    Breathing that earnest prayer,
My heart went in with the jewel,
    A present for maiden Clare.

NEW-YEAR'S EVE.

WITH a bottle and a friend
   — Friend is Tom and bottle Sherry —
I shall now begin and end
This brief space where two years blend,
   Wondrous wise and merry.

Never yet was there a woe
   That had not a pleasure pressing
Close upon its heels; and so
Through the Old and New we go,
   Each at some time blessing.

Though the Old Year brought to me
   Little joy and much of sorrow,
In the New I hope to be
Happier: my joys, you see,
   Always come — to-morrow.

New-Year's Eve.

So, as New-Year's Eve doth end,
   Tom, and I, and golden Sherry
— Finest wine and oldest friend —
Kill the space where two years blend,
   Making wondrous merry.

JUBILATE.

GRAY distance hid each shining sail,
    By ruthless breezes borne from me;
And, lessening, fading, faint and pale,
    My ships went forth to sea.

Where misty breakers rose and fell
    I stood and sorrowed hopelessly;
For every wave had tales to tell
    Of wrecks far out at sea.

To-day, a song is on my lips:
    Earth seems a paradise to me:
For God is good, and, lo, my ships
    Are coming home from sea!

THE MATRON YEAR.

I.

THE leaves that made our forest pathways shady
    Begin to rustle down upon the breeze;
The year is fading, like a stately lady
    Who lays aside her youthful vanities:
Yet, while the memory of her beauty lingers,
    She cannot wear the livery of the old,
So Autumn comes, to paint with frosty fingers
    Some leaves with hues of crimson and of gold.

II.

The Matron's voice filled all the hills and valleys
    With full-toned music, when the leaves were young;
While now, in forest dells and garden-alleys,
    A chirping, reedy song at eve is sung;

Yet sometimes, too, when sunlight gilds the morning,
    A carol bursts from some half-naked tree,
As if, her slow but sure decadence scorning,
    She woke again the olden melody.

III.

With odorous May-buds, sweet as youthful pleasures,
    She made her beauty bright and debonair :
But now, the sad earth yields no floral treasures,
    And twines no roses for the Matron's hair :
Still can she not all lovely things surrender ;
    Right regal is her drapery even now, —
Gold, purple, green, inwrought with every splendor,
    And clustering grapes in garlands on her brow !

IV.

In June, she brought us tufts of fragrant clover
    Rife with the wild bee's cheery monotone,
And, when the earliest bloom was past and over,
    Offered us sweeter scents from fields new-mown :

Now, upland orchards yield, with pattering
   laughter,
Their red-cheeked bounty to the groaning wain,
And heavy-laden racks go creeping after,
   Piled high with sheaves of golden-bearded grain.

V.

Erelong, when all to love and life are clinging,
   And festal holly shines on every wall,
Her knell shall be the New-Year bells, outringing;
   The drifted snow, her stainless burial-pall:
She fades and fails, but proudly and sedately,
   This Matron Year, who has such largess given,
Her brow still tranquil, and her presence stately,
   As one who, losing earth, holds fast to heaven!

REQUIESCAM.

GIVE me, when I die,
    A grave among the corn and clover.
Let me peaceful lie
    In some field, with forests nigh,
Where the blossoms bending over
    Mingle sigh for sigh
With ever rustling leaves
Whispering to the rustling sheaves.

    Let the tall grass wave
    High above my grave,
And strew, each fall, their treasures o'er me;
    Leaves of gold, and brown,
    Softly floating down,
Or driven wildly onward, when 't is stormy.

    O give me not a tomb
White, and marble-cold, and dreary,

Requiescam.

In the churchyard's gloom !
Rather, when I 'm weary,
Let me lie at rest
   'Neath the clover, growing fair,
   In the warm, sunshiny air,
With its thready tendrils twining round my breast.

So, tranquil be my sleep,
When the hazy, slanting beams
   Rest on forest, vale, and steep,
Through long, summer afternoons
   Be my slumber still and deep.
Let the new and waning moons
Come, and go, and bring me dreams.

IN THE DARK.

[While this book was passing through the press, a fortunate accident placed in my possession the original manuscript of this, the last poem that Arnold wrote. It was written within a few days of his death, when the shadow of the night that knows no earthly dawn was already closing around him. — W. W.]

ALL moveless stand the ancient cedar-trees
    Along the drifted sand-hills where they grow;
And from the dark west comes a wandering breeze,
    And waves them to and fro.

A murky darkness lies along the sand,
    Where bright the sunbeams of the morning shone;
And the eye vainly seeks, by sea and land,
    Some light to rest upon.

In the Dark.

No large, pale star its glimmering vigil keeps;
    An inky sea reflects an inky sky;
And the dark river, like a serpent, creeps
    To where its black piers lie.

Strange, salty odors through the darkness steal,
    And through the dark the ocean-thunders roll.
Thick darkness gathers, stifling, till I feel
    Its weight upon my soul!

I stretch my hands out in the empty air;
    I strain my eyes into the heavy night;
Blackness of darkness!... Father, hear my prayer...
    Grant me to see the light!

THE END.

www.ingramcontent.com/pod-product-compliance
Lightning Source LLC
Chambersburg PA
CBHW020253170426
43202CB00008B/350